This Is a Let's-Read-and-Find-Out Science Book®

Joanna Cole   illustrated by Aliki

EVOLUTION

Thomas Y. Crowell   New York

Other Recent Let's-Read-and-Find-Out Science Books® You Will Enjoy

Danger—Icebergs! · Rockets and Satellites · The Planets in Our Solar System · The Moon Seems to Change · Ant Cities · Get Ready for Robots! · Gravity Is a Mystery · Snow Is Falling · Journey into a Black Hole · What Makes Day and Night · Air Is All Around You · Turtle Talk · What the Moon Is Like · Hurricane Watch · Sunshine Makes the Seasons · My Visit to the Dinosaurs · The BASIC Book · Bits and Bytes · Germs Make Me Sick! · Flash, Crash, Rumble, and Roll · Volcanoes · Dinosaurs Are Different · What Happens to a Hamburger · Meet the Computer · How to Talk to Your Computer · Comets · Rock Collecting · Is There Life in Outer Space? · All Kinds of Feet · Flying Giants of Long Ago · Rain and Hail · Why I Cough, Sneeze, Shiver, Hiccup, & Yawn · You Can't Make a Move Without Your Muscles · The Sky Is Full of Stars · Digging Up Dinosaurs · No Measles, No Mumps for Me

The *Let's-Read-and-Find-Out Science Book* series was originated by Dr. Franklyn M. Branley, Astronomer Emeritus and former Chairman of the American Museum–Hayden Planetarium, and was formerly co-edited by him and Dr. Roma Gans, Professor Emeritus of Childhood Education, Teachers College, Columbia University. For a complete catalog of Let's-Read-and-Find-Out Science Books, write to Thomas Y. Crowell Junior Books, Harper & Row, Publishers, Inc., 10 East 53rd Street, New York, NY 10022.

Evolution
Text copyright © 1987 by Joanna Cole
Illustrations copyright © 1987 by Aliki Brandenberg
All rights reserved. No part of this book may be used or reproduced in any manner whatsoever without written permission except in the case of brief quotations embodied in critical articles and reviews. Printed in the United States of America. For information address Thomas Y. Crowell Junior Books, 10 East 53rd Street, New York, N.Y. 10022. Published simultaneously in Canada by Fitzhenry & Whiteside Limited, Toronto.
Typography by Al Cetta
1 2 3 4 5 6 7 8 9 10
First Edition

Library of Congress Cataloging-in-Publication Data
Cole, Joanna.
  Evolution.

  (Let's-read-and-find-out science book)
  Summary: Describes, using evidence found in fossil layers, how one-cell organisms evolved into complex plants and animals.
  1. Evolution—Juvenile literature. [1. Evolution. 2. Fossils] I. Aliki, ill. II. Title. III. Series.
QH367.1.C65 1987   575   87-638
ISBN 0-690-04596-4
ISBN 0-690-04598-0 (lib. bdg.)

Once a farmer was digging in a field.
He found a rock that looked like a bone.

Another time, a child found a stone shaped like a seashell.

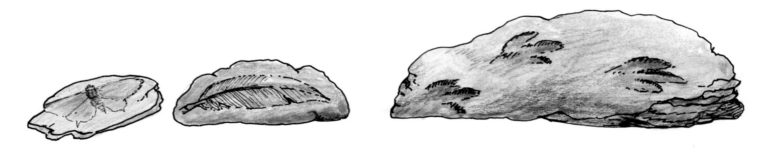

People have found rocks with the shapes of leaves and insects pressed into them, and even rocks with footprints in them.

Rocks and stones that look like living things have always
puzzled people.

People wondered, are they accidents?

Are they rocks that just happen to look like living things,
the way a cloud sometimes looks like an animal?

Or, they wondered, could these rocks be the remains of real plants
and animals?

Throughout history, many rocks like this have been found.
Scientists have studied them closely.
The scientists can tell that they really are the remains of
plants and animals.

These plants and animals lived thousands and millions,
even billions, of years ago.
And over the years, their remains have hardened into rock.
Scientists call these rocks fossils, which comes from a word that
means "dug up."

Most fossils are found in rock strata, or layers.
These layers were laid down long ago as mud or sand.
Over time, the mud or sand was pressed into hard rock.
Strata of rock were formed one on top of another
like layers in a layer cake.
The lower layers were laid down first and are the oldest.
The upper layers are the newest.

Sometimes scientists can test rocks to find out how old they are.
They can tell which rocks are oldest—
even if layers were scrambled by an earthquake.

ROCK STRATA

SCRAMBLED STRATA

About two hundred years ago, an engineer in England named
William Smith was in charge of building a large canal.
As the workers dug, they uncovered rock strata.

Smith noticed that there were fossils in the strata.

And he noticed something else.

Each layer had its own kinds of fossils.

Certain kinds of plant and animal fossils were always together
in one layer.

Scientists have noticed the same thing in rock layers everywhere in the world.
In the very oldest layers, the only fossils are traces of very simple plants and animals.
These plants and animals were made of just a single cell.
In the newer layers, there are fossils of more complex animals and plants.
The animals were made of many cells and had shells or skeletons and different body parts.
The plants had different parts too—
leaves, roots, stems, and flowers.

Most single cells are so tiny they can only be seen with a microscope.

Millions of years ago	PERIOD			ERA
2	QUATERNARY		Humans	CENOZOIC
65	TERTIARY		Spread of mammals Many flowering plants Many birds	CENOZOIC
136	CRETACEOUS		Last dinosaurs First flowering plants	MESOZOIC
193	JURASSIC		Many dinosaurs First birds	MESOZOIC
225	TRIASSIC		First dinosaurs First small mammals	MESOZOIC
280	PERMIAN		Many reptiles Many insects Cone-bearing trees	LATE PALEOZOIC
300	(Pennsylvanian) CARBONIFEROUS		First reptiles Tree ferns	LATE PALEOZOIC
345	(Mississippian)		Many amphibians	LATE PALEOZOIC
395	DEVONIAN		First bony fishes First amphibians First insects	EARLY PALEOZOIC
435	SILURIAN		First land plants First fishes with jaws	EARLY PALEOZOIC
500	ORDOVICIAN		Jawless fishes (first animals with backbones)	EARLY PALEOZOIC
570	CAMBRIAN		First animals with shells Seaweeds	EARLY PALEOZOIC
4000 (4 billion)	PRECAMBRIAN		First living things (one-celled plants and animals)	

A period is made up of many, many rock layers.

13

The order of the fossil layers tells us something important.
It tells the story of how life developed on earth.

When life began, there were only very simple plants and animals,
such as one-celled algae and bacteria.

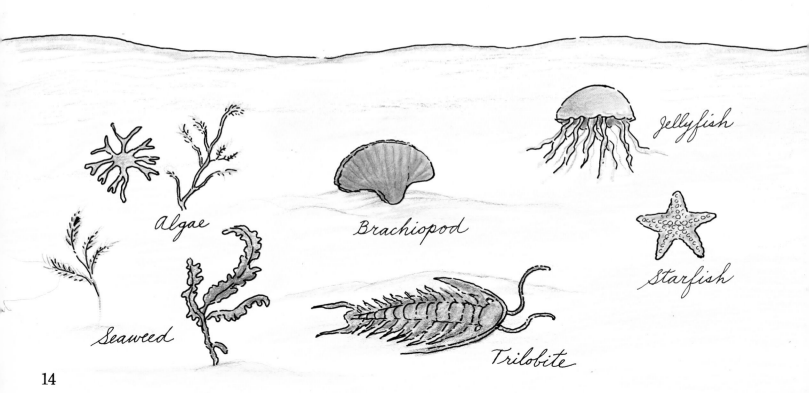

Algae

Seaweed

Brachiopod

Trilobite

Jellyfish

Starfish

As time went on, more complex living things appeared,
such as jellyfish and sponges.
As more time passed, new kinds of plants and animals
appeared that were more and more complex, and more and more
different from one another.

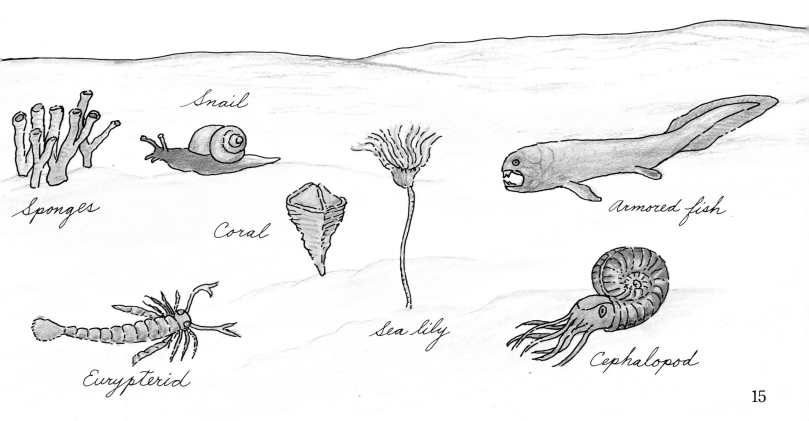

Snail

Sponges

Coral

Sea lily

Armored fish

Eurypterid

Cephalopod

Some of the older kinds of living things survived through the ages.
Many others died out—they became extinct.
But all the time new kinds of plants and animals were
coming into being.
Life was growing and changing!

Dragonfly

Lobe-fin fish

Land plants

Lungfish

Stereosaurus

Horseshoe crab

Pteranodon

Archaeopteryx

Bird

Woolly mammoth

Dinosaur

Ramapithecus

Human

Flowering plants

Shrew

Saber-toothed tiger

Horseshoe crab

Snail

Fishes

Crocodile

Seaweed

17

Where did the new kinds of living things come from?
Scientists today think that the new animals developed—
evolved—from the older ones.
The older kinds of living things were the ancestors of the new ones.

More than a hundred years ago, a scientist named Charles Darwin
wrote a book that became famous.
The book showed how all plants and animals could have developed
from earlier, simpler living things.
This idea is called *evolution*.

H.M.S. BEAGLE

On the Origin of Species by Means of Natural Selection
CHARLES DARWIN

It is hard to imagine one kind of animal evolving into another kind.
After all, no single animal can change itself into another
kind of animal.
Your dog cannot become a cat.
And no fish in your bowl will ever turn into a frog.
But scientists think that over millions of years a whole new kind
of plant or animal can develop from an earlier kind.

An example of this is the evolution of amphibians.
Amphibians—animals such as frogs and salamanders—
probably evolved from a kind of fish called a lobe-fin, which
lived more than 350 million years ago.
The lobe-fins had strong fins for crawling along the bottoms
of streams.

They had gills like other fish for breathing underwater.
But they also had simple lungs.
If their stream dried up, lobe-fins were able to breathe air
for a while.
They could crawl over mud on their strong fins and find a new
pool or stream.

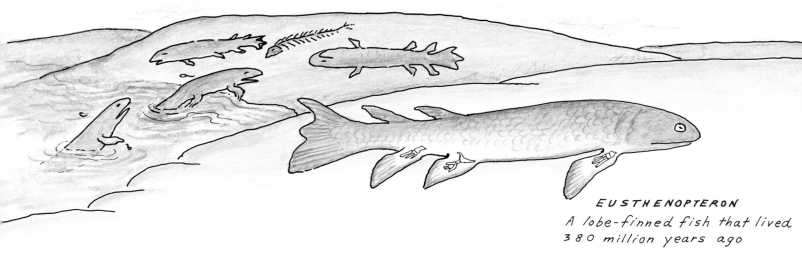

EUSTHENOPTERON
A lobe-finned fish that lived
380 million years ago

How could these fish have evolved into amphibians?

Perhaps some lobe-fins were born that were especially good at living on land.

Maybe these new lobe-fins had extra-strong fins.

And extra-large lungs.

Around this same time, the weather probably became drier in the lobe-fins' part of the world.

Streams dried up and stayed dry longer.

Many lobe-fins died, but the new lobe-fins survived.

They passed on their extra-strong fins and their extra-large lungs to some of their offspring.

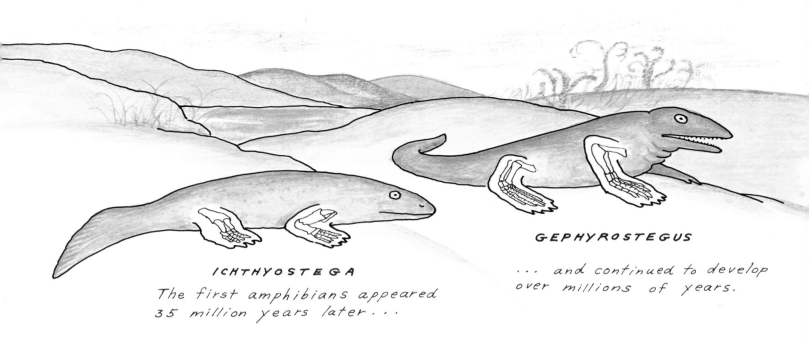

ICHTHYOSTEGA

The first amphibians appeared 35 million years later...

GEPHYROSTEGUS

... and continued to develop over millions of years.

Then offspring were born that had even stronger fins.

Over time, the fins became more and more like legs.

The new creatures lost their gills and became even better at breathing air.

The original lobe-fin fish eventually died out.

But the descendents of lobe-fins were the first amphibians.

23

In a similar way, amphibians were the ancestors of reptiles—
animals such as dinosaurs, snakes, lizards, and crocodiles.
Reptiles then gave rise to the first birds.

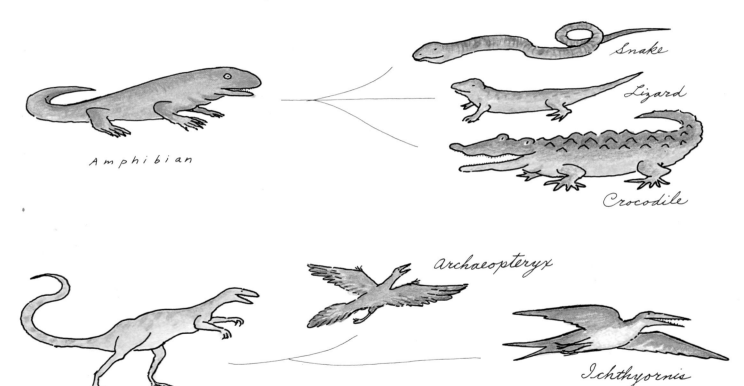

Amphibian

Snake

Lizard

Crocodile

Archaeopteryx

Ichthyornis

COELUROSAUR (dinosaur)
Reptile

Reptiles were also the ancestors of the first mammals, which
were shrew-like creatures.
From these, all other mammals evolved—
dogs, cats, mice, horses, whales, monkeys, and apes,
even human beings.

Mammal
ancestor

There was once a creature that was the direct ancestor of both apes and human beings.

Apes evolved in one direction, and humans evolved in another.

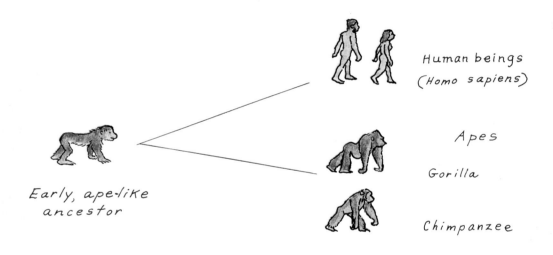

Early, ape-like ancestor

Human beings (Homo sapiens)

Apes

Gorilla

Chimpanzee

Apes are forest-dwelling plant eaters.

They do not walk upright.

Compared to humans, apes have small brains.

And wild apes do not use language.

Human beings evolved quite differently.
They walked upright, and their brains became larger and larger.
They made tools and weapons.
They began to communicate with language.

AUSTRALOPITHECUS	HOMO HABILIS	HOMO ERECTUS	NEANDERTHAL (Homo sapiens neanderthalensis)	MODERN HUMAN (Homo sapiens sapiens)
Lived from 3,500,000 years ago to 1,300,000 years ago	Lived from 2,000,000 years ago to 1,500,000 years ago	Lived from 1,700,000 years ago to 250,000 years ago	Lived from 150,000 years ago to 32,000 years ago	Lived from about 40,000 years ago to the present

Cro- Magnon people
(modern *Homo* sapiens who lived in France 40,000 years ago)

No one saw evolution happen.
It happened over billions of years.
We cannot even imagine such a long time.
But we can "read" the story told by the fossils.
And, like detectives, we can figure out how life evolved
on Earth—from the first simple cells to all the complex plants and
animals of today.